The
Garland Library
of
War and Peace

The
Garland Library
of
War and Peace

Under the General Editorship of
Blanche Wiesen Cook, *John Jay College, C.U.N.Y.*
Sandi E. Cooper, *Richmond College, C.U.N.Y.*
Charles Chatfield, *Wittenberg University*

Callinicus
A Defence of Chemical Warfare

by
John Burdon Sanderson
J. B. S. Haldane

with a new introduction
for the Garland Edition by

Seymour L. Chapin

Garland Publishing, Inc., New York & London
1972

Library of Congress Cataloging in Publication Data

Haldane, John Burdon Sanderson, 1892-1964.
    Callinicus; a defence of chemical warfare.

    (The Garland library of war and peace)
    Original ed. issued in series: To-day and to-morrow
series.
    1. Chemical warfare. I. Title. II. Series.
III. Series: To-day and to-morrow series.
UG447.H3 1972   358'.34   78-148366
ISBN 0-8240-0461-2

Printed in the United States of America

Introduction

According to the recent and impressive six-volume study of The Problem of Chemical and Biological Warfare by the Stockholm International Peace Research Institute, this short book by J.B.S. Haldane "even today remains the most forceful statement of the humanity argument for chemical weapons." That characterization, involving no claims that Haldane's words were the first or the last on this subject, seems essentially sound.

Clearly the idea that science could make important contributions to warfare did not originate with Haldane. One can find centuries earlier expressions of this general concept, while even the American Civil War saw the advocacy of the position that specifically chemical weapons — and more particularly incapacitating gas — could, in the future, eliminate death and injury during wartime. But these arguments dealt only with possibilities, for modern chemical warfare became a reality only with the German release of a cloud of chlorine gas at Ypres in April 1915.

There was a twofold Allied reaction to this violation of the 1899 Hague Declaration, according to which the contracting powers agreed "to abstain from the use of projectiles the sole object of which is the *diffusion of asphyxiating or deleterious gases." One of these was fully predictable: it was the portrayal of this action not only as proof of the duplicity of the Hun, but as an act of inhumanity contrary to all codes of civilized behavior and even as another instance of a German atrocity. The Germans, for their part, responded by maintaining that gas was a weapon which, in addition to being legitimate, could be regarded as far more humane than high explosive shells.*

In light of their propagandistic use of the German utilization of gas, the other Allied reaction might be considered unexpected. It consisted, in essence, of a tacit acceptance of what the Hun had done. Rather than devoting themselves to formal protests, the Allies dedicated themselves, first, to developing defense against German gases and, second, to preparing their own offensive weapons. Thus, at its end World War I was about 50 percent chemical. Whatever qualms military leaders and others might have had regarding the initiation of this type of warfare were submerged under a rising tide of demonstrated efficiency.

Some figures bearing on the matter of efficacy seem appropriate. It is not necessary to present these either in any great detail or with regard to all the belligerents. Indeed, one need offer only the casualty figures of the American Expeditionary Forces since these reflect the conditions prevailing during that stage of the war when both the employment of gas had become a rather standard part of any attack and the perfected protective devices were in equally common use.

Briefly, these American forces experienced 258,338 battle casualties. Of this number, 34,249, or 13.3%, were killed outright or died on the field of battle; only 200 of them died from gas. The remaining casualties, 224,089, were removed to hospitals. Of these, 70,552, some 27.3%, were due to gas. But, and here one enters into considerations fraught with future significance, of that large number of casualties, only 1,221 died. Thus, when one combines the battlefield and hospital figures, it turns out that some 1,421 American soldiers died from exposure to gas and that this is under 2% of those affected.

It appears, therefore, that gas was an effective means of inflicting casualties on one's enemies; large numbers of men could be removed from combat in this way, while, importantly, their physical surroundings suffered little or no damage. At the same time, most of the men could be returned to the front after a period of hospitalization. Not all of them, of course, for, in addition to those who died, some were permanently disabled. But the number of these and the aftereffects from which they suffered have been greatly exaggerated, thanks to the notoriety surrounding the use of gas. It is probably quite true, as one medical officer has said, that gas has been — incorrectly — "credited with more dire iniquities than have ever been associated with any other weapon."

These figures made it possible, in the immediate postwar years, to revert to the German wartime argument of the humaneness of this new weapon. That concept now had concrete support. Moreover, it had concrete aims.

There were two principal groups of advocates of the resuscitated humane position at this time. One was the body of military veterans of chemical branches who argued for the continuation of their services in the peacetime armies. The other was made up of representatives of chemical industries – and particularly, of course, the dyestuffs segment thereof – who wanted their war-created plants and techniques protected by tariff barriers against an expected resurgence of the prewar German domination. Both achieved their goals, at least partially. That they did so, however, was far more a result of their playing upon established fears of gas warfare and future instances of unpreparedness therein than of their utilization of the theme of that warfare's humanity. Indeed, the latter approach was soon washed aside by a wide wave of sentiment in favor of some form of chemical disarmament.

The most important result of this new current was the incorporation of an anti-gas article in the Washington Treaty of 1922. Thanks to non-ratification by the French, which action had nothing to do with its gas warfare provisions, the Treaty was never enforced. Its existence did, however, inspire three subsequent agreements. And, more importantly for the purposes of this introduction, it accelerated and redirected the consideration of this problem that had been underway in the League of Nations for over two years; specifically, it engendered the creation of a special Sub-Committee on Chemical Warfare whose work program called for the addressing of a questionnaire to a number of experts in bacteriological and chemical fields requesting their opinions on the effects which could be produced by attacks featuring weapons from those fields.

Although the number of experts approached in this way is unknown, some eight individuals responded. They were of diverse nationality, including two Italians and two Americans and one representative each from France, Belgium, Denmark, and Poland. It was on the basis of their answers that a full report was submitted to the League near the end of July 1924.

This report's consideration of the effects of gas on human life was based almost exclusively on the experience and aftermath of World War I, and proceeded, in good scientific fashion, by means of the physiological characterization of the several agents that had then been employed. More interesting, therefore, was its attention to the "Possible Effects of New Discoveries," a consideration necessitated by some scientists' insistence that "No guaranty can be given that new substances will not be discovered which affect other functions of the body." With regard to the effects of gas on a country's sources of wealth, the report utilized the views of one of the American experts, who had written that these "would be indirect and would be due either to the paralyzing action on the human element, as, for example, the shutting-down of factories through the gassing of the surroundings, so as to render them unapproachable to workmen, or to the action of incendiary materials. . . ." Since the first of these outcomes would take place where "means of protection were not employed," the report next considered the efficacy of such means. Thus, masks, their manner of operation, and the need for training in their use were discussed and reported to be adequate for the concentrations of gas that had been used in the past and for those likely to be used in the present. The lack of protective means against blistering agents and the possibility that masks might prove insufficient in the future were, however, areas of concern. Closely connected with these problems was that of the use of the chemical arm against civilians. The report recognized that the distinction between combatants and those not directly engaged in fighting was becoming more difficult to draw — or, at least, that it might not be retained in the future. And, since "an unscrupulous belligerent may not see much difference between the use of poison gas against troops in the field and its use against the centers from which those troops draw the sinews of war," the prospects for protecting the civilian element were felt to be bleak: "To furnish a whole population with gas masks would seem almost impracticable, and methods for collective protection have yet to be proved efficient; yet, short of that, and especially in the absence of any knowledge as to where the attack was to be delivered, no complete protection could be secured." These points entered into the report's summary of the state of expert opinion on the question of the effects of gas. Also placed there were those remarks of the scientists which touched upon that most difficult aspect of any scheme for chemical disarmament, namely, the ease of convertibility from peaceful to war-directed chemical production. With all of these things in mind, the report concluded with a warning: "Noting, therefore, on the one hand the ever-increasing and varying machinery of science as applied to warfare, and on the other, the vital danger to which a nation would expose itself if it were lulled into security by over-confidence in international treaties and conventions, suddenly to find itself defenseless against a new arm, it is . . . essential that all nations should realize to the full the terrible nature of the danger which threatens them."

I have devoted this rather large amount of attention to a rather obscure League of Nations report (the equivalent statement which issued from the United Nations in July 1969 did not even mention the existence of its forty-five-year-old counterpart) because of the fact that Haldane's book

may be seen as the most important specific reaction
to it. *Indeed, it is at least possible — especially since
British scientists were notable by their absence from
the group of League experts — that Haldane may have
been asked for his opinion by the special
Sub-Committee, and that* Callinicus *was his answer.
That "J.B.S.," as he was already coming to be
popularly known, might have been requested to
present his views is not at all far-fetched. Born the
son of the well-known British physiologist, John
Scott Haldane, in 1892, J.B.S. had early joined his
father in mine, diving, and submarine investigations,
had co-authored a scientific paper with him as early
as 1912, and shown an original flair for mathematical
genetics in an effort of his own in the same year, his
first at Oxford. His very promising future was
interrupted by World War I, service in which he found
in many ways enjoyable. Significantly, however, he
was withdrawn from his line activities in order once
again to aid his father, this time in the development
of the respirators designed to save Allied troops from
future destruction at the hands of further German gas
attacks following upon the initial use at Ypres. He
thereafter returned to the line, only to be gassed and
wounded by a shell splinter himself. A year of
instructing followed his recuperation, after which
period he passed the remainder of the war in
Mesopotamia.*

*After the war J.B.S. returned to an Oxford
Fellowship and studies in physiology in which his*

penchant for self-experimentation earned him a growing fame. This work in turn caused him to be called to a Readership in Biochemistry at Cambridge in 1923. There he stayed for a decade making notable offerings to the study of enzymes and contributing significantly to the development of the field of genetics. Of far greater interest here, however, was his effort to explain science to the layman, an activity which resulted in a number of brilliant popular essays which are one of his main claims to fame.

His first important venture of this sort was his 1924 piece entitled Daedalus, or Science and the Future. *Concentrating on future biological discoveries and enlarging upon the possibilities of ectogenesis, or birth outside the human body, this work, although undoubtedly upsetting many individuals, did not strike at established opinions. It was quite otherwise with* Callinicus.

While the preparation of this small book as a participant among the League experts seems not unreasonable from the standpoint of Haldane's background and present activities, there is really no evidence to support this suggestion. On the other hand, the fact that it was originally offered as a lecture in August 1924, only weeks after the report to the League, does at least add credence to the idea that it might be considered an answer to that report. It represents, as it were, a kind of minority expert opinion. Indeed, perhaps the major significance of this statement from one of England's leading biochemists was its clear demonstration that, despite the implication of the League report to the contrary, scientists did not view the subject of chemical and bacteriological warfare with universal alarm.

Haldane differed from his learned international colleagues, for example, by facing the future more calmly, both because he read the lessons of World War I in a more favorable light and because he did not think that new developments in this field would vary greatly from that past experience. As with the earlier proponents of the humanitarianism of gas, he supported the first of these positions by reference to actual casualty figures. He also went beyond them, however, and invoked his personal experience, not only with a favorable contrast between his wartime gassing as opposed to his shell wound, but as well with peacetime asphyxiations "to the point of unconsciousness" undergone in his self-experimentation programs. As to the second position, he simply did not think that any truly "new" gas would appear. To the contrary, he argued that "the use of mustard gas in war on the largest possible scale would render it less expensive of life and property, shorter and more dependent on brains rather than numbers."

Such an anticipated extensive use of the gas weapon foresaw the possibility of its utilization against civilians in London and other large English towns. His answer was the provision, thought impracticable by the League's temporary commissioners, of gas masks to those populations "and the

14

instruction of school-children in their use." That action, he felt, would be "one of the very few military measures which could hardly be regarded as provocative by the most ardent of foreign militarists or British pacifists."

Haldane had contempt for the approaches of pacifists because, while he shared their objection to war, he doubted "whether by objecting to it we are likely to avoid it in the future, however lofty our motives or disinterested our conduct." To forbid the use of chemical substances he considered "a piece of sentimentalism as cruel as it is ridiculous." Moreover, it was folly — as witness the fate of the Hague Declaration. Nor did the more recent Washington agreement fare any better, being characterized by him as at least in part the result of "the complete and shameful ignorance of most of the politicians and many of the soldiers who took part in the Conference." Not that there was much to be hoped for from the latter, who, after all, were attached to cruel and obsolete killing machines by a long-established — but long-outdated — tradition. Indeed, Haldane saw what he called the Bayardism of the military as one of the major obstacles to the further development of a humanitarian weapons technology.

In advancing arguments of these last types, Haldane found himself on a common ground with the report to the League. As with it, Haldane's real theme — and his major plea — was for greater knowledge.

The aim of Callinicus, *however, was to dissipate rather than to precipitate fear.* He recognized that "with gas or rays or microbes one has an altogether different state of affairs" in which incomprehensibility has always produced "a great moral effect." But he further stated that "as long as we permit ourselves to be afraid of the novel and unknown, there will be a very great temptation to use novel and unknown weapons against us."

It should be noted that Haldane's attempt to allay fears on this score remained fruitless. As opposed to his specific answer to it, the general reaction to the League report was a greatly increased interest in the whole subject of poison gas and a new effort at international control over chemical warfare which resulted in the Geneva Protocol of 1925. Although his immediate feelings about that agreement are unknown, it may be safely assumed that he regarded it as a rather useless endeavor. Certainly he felt that way in the 1930s when one of his activities — associated with his ever greater Leftist leanings — was the offering of advice to the Spanish Republican Government on what gases the Franco Air Force was most likely to use and what precautions should be taken. Although that use did not materialize, Haldane thereafter became an outspoken advocate, in essays prepared for the Daily Worker and other writings, of air raid precautions for England, including anti-gas measures, in preparation for the assault he came to expect from Hitler's Germany. His prophecy in that *direction proved erroneous too, although undoubt-edly J.B.S. would have claimed that English preparedness and retaliatory ability were far more important in invalidating it than simple adherence to a paper protocol.*

It perhaps should be mentioned in conclusion that Callinicus *had erred in another of its arguments. Unknown to Haldane — and to the Allies until after World War II — Germany had developed a new gas weapon. One can only speculate on how the existence of nerve gas might have altered the positions maintained by J.B.S. My guess is that he would have energetically refused to change, claiming that the bases of his humanitarian argument remained intact. As suggested at the outset of this introduction,* Callinicus *remains forceful today.*

Seymour L. Chapin
Department of History
California State College
Los Angeles

CALLINICUS

A DEFENCE OF CHEMICAL WARFARE

OTHER VOLUMES IN THE
TO-DAY AND TO-MORROW SERIES

DAEDALUS, or Science and the Future
By J. B. S. Haldane

ICARUS, or The Future of Science
By Bertrand Russell, F.R.S.

THE MONGOL IN OUR MIDST
By F. G. Crookshank, M.D.
New light on Man and the Great Apes
Fully Illustrated

WIRELESS POSSIBILITIES
By Prof. A. M. Low
Wireless in war, crime, business, and pleasure
With 4 Diagrams

TANTALUS, or The Future of Man
By F. C. S. Schiller
Man has still the primitive animal passions. He
will destroy himself, unless . . .

THE PASSING OF THE PHANTOMS
By Professor Patten
Experiments on animals' intelligence throw light
on the evolution of morals in men and animals.

LYSISTRATA, or Woman and the Future
By Anthony M. Ludovici

PERSEUS, or Of Dragons
By H. F. Scott Stokes, M.A.

NARCISSUS, An Anatomy of Clothes
By Gerald Heard

E. P. DUTTON & COMPANY

CALLINICUS

A DEFENCE OF CHEMICAL WARFARE

BY

J. B. S. HALDANE

*Sir William Dunn Reader in Biochemistry,
Cambridge University
Author of "Daedalus or Science and the
Future," etc.*

NEW YORK
E. P. DUTTON & COMPANY
681 FIFTH AVE.

CALLINICUS

THE public mind has to a large extent reacted against the opinions impressed on it during the war by official propaganda. Some of these have been overcome by counter-propaganda in the Press and on the platform; others have been dropped because they led to effects which, though admirable during a war, were undesirable in peace-time. But, as chemical warfare will not assume importance until the outbreak of the next serious war, and figures on the programme of no party, people still think about it as they were told to think by the newspapers during the Great War. Now, I am to some extent a chemist, so I can no more be expected to be impartial in my estimate of the value of chemistry than a politician or a clergyman can be expected to give an unbiassed view of the value of politics or religion. I can only plead that, unlike the average clergyman or politician, I have warned my audience in advance, and shall attempt (though no doubt vainly) to be impartial.

A few of my hearers hold the view that, while war in itself is a noble occupation, the use of poisonous gas is an innovation as cruel as it is unsoldierly. The majority are probably pacifists in the sense that they prefer almost any peace to almost any war, support the League of Nations or other devices for the prevention of international strife, and look askance at preparations for future warfare, more particularly for future chemical warfare. If so, I certainly share their objection to war, but I doubt whether by objecting to it we are likely to avoid it in future, however lofty our motives or disinterested our conduct. War will be prevented only by a scientific study of its causes, such as has prevented most epidemic diseases. For many centuries people had guessed that epidemic diseases constituted a punishment for human misconduct of some kind. They tried to prevent them by prayer and almsgiving. Christians gave up washing, Hindus liberated rats captured d u r i n g plague-epidemics. Religious orders and priests of the church gave the most magnificent examples of self-sacrifice in times of pestilence. But that was not the way

[3]

in which pestilences can be prevented. Besides good intentions, a special type of accurate thinking was needed. We have not yet made a scientific study of the causes of war, and, until we do, may expect more wars. If we are to have more wars, I prefer that my country should be on the winning side. That is why I am speaking on warfare to my fellow-countrymen.

In general, pacifists are a very great military advantage to Britain. On the outbreak of war the large majority of them become intensely patriotic, whereas beforehand they lead our own military authorities and also those of our potential allies and enemies to underestimate our strength. This keeps us out of some wars, and leads to our showing unsuspected power in others.

[4]

CHEMICAL WARFARE

After a few years of war, when the originally bellicose politicians like Lord Lansdowne are getting tired, ex-pacifists like Lloyd George and Pitt have just got into their stride. The national staying-power is thus greatly increased. I need hardly remark that future governments will not enter on war without first persuading the vast majority of the people of its justice. This appears to be a relatively simple process under modern conditions.

At the present moment, however, pacifists are combining with the less competent soldiers in an attempt to check the progress of chemical warfare. This I believe to be neither in our national nor in the international interest.

Until 1915 the soldier's business was

to push or throw pieces of metal at the enemy. Various devices had been employed for throwing them fast or far, and some of them threw other pieces on arrival at their destination, thanks, in the main, to the genius of the unforgotten Major-General Shrapnel. It is true that early in the eighth century A.D. the appropriately named Syrian Callinicus had prolonged the life of the Eastern Roman Empire for another 750 years and saved a large part of Christendom from Mahommedan domination by his invention of "Greek fire," an inflammable liquid which was, however, later superseded by gunpowder. In the fifteenth century the defenders of Belgrade against the Turks had hit upon a similar device, under the direct inspiration, it was claimed, of the

Holy Ghost, but these weapons had fallen into desuetude, their effect being largely psychological.

Chemical warfare had been so far foreseen by statesmen that in 1907 the signatories of the Hague Conference agreed to renounce the use of projectiles the sole object of which was the diffusion of asphyxiating or harmful gases. They were thus debarred from using lachrymatory gas, the most humane weapon ever invented; but permitted to discharge gas from cylinders on the ground, an exceedingly cruel practice. This regulation was well meant, but the path to August, 1914, was paved with good intentions. In 1914 none of the great powers had made any preparation for poison-gas warfare, and it was not till April 22nd, 1915, more than eight

[7]

months after the beginning of the war,
that the Germans began its use.

During the war, twenty-five different
poisonous weapons were employed. Of
these only three are gases at ordinary
temperatures, and can be discharged
from cylinders in which they are stored
under pressure. The remainder are
liquids which gradually evaporate,
yielding a poisonous vapour, or solids
which are poisonous in the form of
smoke.

These poisonous substances so far
used fall into four classes according to
their effect on men. First come gases
and vapours which are poisonous when
breathed, but have no effect on the skin,
and affect the eyes or nose only when
present in concentrations which are
poisonous to the lungs. They can all

[8]

be kept out by respirators, and were of military value only against unprotected troops, or in local surprise-action. This group, which included chlorine and phosgene, are probably almost as obsolete as muzzle-loading cannon.

A second group are poisonous only in very high concentrations, but irritate the eyes when present in amounts so small that one part in five million may render a man blind with weeping in a few seconds. There is no evidence, so far as I know, that anyone was killed or even permanently blinded by these substances; but they had a great momentary effect. They can be kept out by respirators, or even goggles.

The third group of poisonous smokes, mostly arsenic compounds,

were little developed during the war.
They are, however, weapons of very
great efficiency, and it is well known
that they would have been used by the
British at any rate on a very extensive
scale in 1919.* In small amounts, these
smokes merely make one sneeze. In
somewhat larger amounts they cause
pain of the most terrific character in
the head and chest. The pain in the
head is described as like that caused
when fresh water gets into the nose
when bathing, but infinitely more
severe. These symptoms are accom-
panied by the most appalling mental
distress and misery. Some soldiers
poisoned by these substances had to be
prevented from committing suicide;

* The American "Lewisite," of which so much
was heard in 1918 and 1919, is a substance of
this class.

others temporarily went raving **mad,** and tried to burrow into the ground to escape from imaginary pursuers. And yet within forty-eight hours the large majority had recovered, and practically none became permanent invalids. These substances, when in the form of smoke, will penetrate any of the respirators used in the late war, though the British box-respirator would stop all but a little of them in the concentrations then used. In future they will probably be used in much larger concentrations and in finer particles than those formed by the German smoke-shells. It is extraordinarily difficult to produce a respirator which will completely stop very fine smoke, for the following reason. In a gas the molecules (or ultimate particles) are moving very rapidly, with speeds of several hundred yards per second, continually colliding and rebounding. A gas molecule, therefore, will probably hit the sides of a fairly narrow passage through which it is drawn. But a smoke particle is moving at a speed measured in inches per second, and is far less likely to hit the wall of the respirator, and be held by its absorbent surface. If we try to make the passages through which air is drawn very narrow, as by sucking in our air through cotton-wool (which will stop most smokes), we find that we have created an appalling resistance to breathing. There is an electrical method of removing smoke-particles completely, but it would probably more than double the weight of respirators, and does not appear to be either water-proof or fool-proof.

CHEMICAL WARFARE

The fourth group, of blistering gases, contains only one substance used during the war, dichlorethyl sulphide, or "mustard gas." This is really a liquid, whose vapour is not only poisonous when breathed, but blisters any part of the skin with which it comes into contact even. To take an example, a drop of the liquid was put on a piece of paper and left for five minutes on a man's sleeve. The vapour penetrated his coat and woollen shirt, causing a blister the effects of which lasted six weeks. And yet evaporation is so slow that ground contaminated by the liquid may remain dangerous for a week. Mustard gas caused more casualties to the British than all other chemical weapons put together.

Such are the weapons which chemistry has given us. It is often asked why chemists cannot produce something which will put our foes comfortably to sleep and allow us to take·them prisoners. The answer is that such substances exist, but that in small amounts they are harmless, in large amounts fatal. It is only over a moderate range of concentrations that their effect is merely stupefying. One has only to think of the familiar case of chloroform vapour, and the skill required to give neither too much nor too little.

It would be logical to speak of explosives under the heading of chemical warfare, but there is curiously little chance of explosives becoming any more effective. We know fairly well the maximum amount of energy which can possibly be got out of a chemical action, and, though explosives might perhaps be made which were about twice as destructive as our best (or worst) to-day, they would probably be far less stable, and therefore less safe to their users.

Of course, if we could utilize the forces which we now know to exist inside the atom, we should have such capacities for destruction that I do not know of any agency other than divine intervention which would save humanity from complete and peremptory annihilation. But the remoteness of the day when we shall use these forces may best be judged by an analogy. Some thousands of years ago someone first realized that the sun, moon and stars were not mere bodies as large as a plate or a house, but very large, and moving very fast. It was an obvious idea that their motions might be exploited in some way. Wise men observed them and hoped, for example, to increase the probability of success in their own enterprises by beginning them when Jupiter was in the ascendant. These attempts were unsuccessful, though far more valuable to humanity than most of the methods successfully employed for the same purposes, such as fraud, violence and corruption. They led to astronomy, and so to all modern physics. We now know that the only probable way of harnessing the kinetic energy of the heavenly bodies is to employ tidal power to create electric currents. But five thousand years ago "hitching one's wagon to a star" was a reasonable project and not a poetic metaphor. The reason we cannot do it is a simple matter of scale. And the reason why we cannot utilize subatomic phenomena is just the same. We cannot make apparatus small enough to disintegrate or fuse atomic nuclei, any more than we can make it large enough to reach to the moon. We can only bombard them with particles of which perhaps one in a million hit, which is like firing keys at a safe-door from a machine-gun a mile away in an attempt to open it. We do occasionally open it, but the process is very uneconomical. It may be asked why we cannot bring our machine-gun nearer, or improve our aim. To do this we should require to construct apparatus on the same infinitesimal scale as the structure of the chemical atom. Now we can arrange atoms into various patterns. For example, we can arrange carbon, hydrogen and oxygen atoms in patterns which constitute the molecules of sugar, glycerine, or alcohol at will. This is called chemical synthesis. We have been doing it by rule-of-thumb methods for thousands of years, and are just beginning to learn a little about it. But even chemical molecules are much too large for our purposes. We can no more ask a chemist to build our apparatus than expect a theatrical scene-painter or a landscape-gardener to do us a miniature. We know very little about the structure of the atom and almost nothing about how to modify it. And the prospect of constructing such an apparatus seems to me to be so remote that, when some successor of mine is lecturing to a party spending a holiday on the moon, it will still be an unsolved (though not, I think, an ultimately insoluble) problem.

To see how chemical weapons are likely to be used in future we must study their employment in the late war. Lachrymatory gas was only once used under ideal conditions—by the Germans in the Argonne in 1915. They captured a fairly extensive French trench system and about 2,400 prisoners, almost all unwounded, but temporarily blind. When they gave the number of prisoners, the French authorities not unnaturally protested that this number was practically equal to the total of their casualties. And this was quite true. The French were unprotected. They were deluged with shells giving off a vapour which temporarily blinded them. They could not even run away. The Germans walked across, removed their rifles, and formed them up in columns which marched back, each led by a German in goggles. In order to make future wars humane it would only be necessary to introduce the two following rules:—

1. No goggles or other eye protection shall be worn;
2. No shells shall be used containing any other substances save ethyl iodo-acetate (or other lachrymatory compound) and a small bursting charge.

Certainly it is unlikely that such rules will ever be adopted, but I do contend that to forbid the use of such substances is a piece of sentimentalism as cruel as it is ridiculous.

[20]

CHEMICAL WARFARE

Gases of the first group were used in clouds discharged from cylinders, sometimes on a front of several miles. They probably caused at least 20,000 casualties among unprotected or inadequately protected British troops. At least a quarter of these died, and that very painfully, in many cases after a struggle for breath lasting several days. On the other hand, of those who did not die almost all recovered completely, and the symptoms of the few who became permanent invalids were mainly nervous. Apart, however, from the extreme terror and agitation produced by the gassing of uneducated people, I regard the type of wound produced by the average shells as, on the whole, more distressing than the pneumonia caused by chlorine or phosgene. Besides being wounded, I have been

[21]

buried alive, and on several occasions in peacetime I have been asphyxiated to the point of unconsciousness. The pain and discomfort arising from the other experiences were utterly negligible compared with those produced by a good septic shell-wound.

The first German cloud-gas attack was in April, 1915, the last in August, 1916, though the British continued them until the end of that year. They gradually became more and more ineffective as the efficiency of the respirators used on both sides increased. The first few German attacks were very well conducted, so far as the liberation of the gas was concerned, as they were arranged by Haber, an extremely competent chemist, who afterwards supervised their production of explosives.

[22]

On the other hand, the German respirators were bad to begin with; and later on were not so good as the British. This was, apparently, because the most competent physiologist in Germany with any knowledge of breathing was a Jew. This fact was quite well known in German physiological circles, but apparently his race prevented the military authorities from employing him. The result was that they were unable to follow up their gas-attacks at all closely, but had to wait till the cloud had passed off, by which time resistance was again possible. That was how the Germans paid for anti-Semitism. It is very probable that it lost them the war, as never again, not even in March, 1918, had they as complete a gap in the Franco-British Western front as during the first gas-attack in April, 1915. It was, indeed, fortunate for the Germans that the Russians were still more anti-Semitic than themselves. Hundreds of thousands of Russian Jews volunteered for service in 1914. They were mostly refused, and in no case granted commissions. They then proceeded to turn their combative instincts into other channels, to the no small advantage of the Germans. If one goes to what is, perhaps, the opposite extreme from Russia, one finds the army of the world's most democratic nation, Australia, commanded by a Jew, Monash, and notes with interest that the Germans regarded the Australian troops as, on the whole, the most formidable, man for man, of all their opponents.

CHEMICAL WARFARE

The other reason why the cloud-gas attacks were indecisive was that the Germans had relatively few reserves to put into the gap they made. Their reserves in April, 1915, were in Poland. If they had trusted their scientific men they could certainly have captured Calais and Boulogne, and probably have annihilated the British Army.

In addition to clouds released from cylinders in the trenches, gas-cylinders were fired from trench-mortars, some hundreds at a time, into the enemy's lines, producing a sudden and dense cloud of gas before the men had time to put on their respirators. But these bombardments, though they caused many casualties, were never decisive, as the cloud-attacks would have been, but for causes which we have discussed.

CALLINICUS

Mustard gas is a very different thing. It was never used to force a decision by breaking the enemy's lines, but to cause him casualties and deny him the use of ground. For, after a given area has been well sprayed with dichlorethyl sulphide from bursting shells for some time, it is death to occupy it without a mask, and the vapour may blister the skin, while anyone touching the ground will be certain of a very serious blister. Someone placed a drop of the liquid on the chair of the director of the British chemical warfare department. He ate his meals off the mantelpiece for a month. The most interesting thing, however, about mustard gas is that, though it caused 150,000 casualties in the British Army alone, less than 4,000 of these (or 1 in 40) died, while only

CHEMICAL WARFARE

about 700 (or 1 in every 200) became permanently unfit. Yet the Washington Conference has solemnly agreed that the signatory powers are not to use this substance against one another, though, of course, they will use such humane weapons as bayonets, shells, and incendiary bombs.

It is worth while attempting to analyse the reasons for this rather curious decision. First, perhaps, we must put the complete and shameful ignorance of most of the politicians and many of the soldiers who took part in the Conference. Their ideas of gas warfare were apparently drawn from the descriptions of the great German cloud-gas attacks of 1915, which killed at least 1 in 4 of their casualties, and were written up on a large scale for recruiting and political purposes. But it is the business of politicians and soldiers, conceivably even of journalists, to know the truth about such matters before coming to decisions, or even impelling others to come to decisions about them.

To this ignorance, however, there was joined one of the most hideous forms of sentimentalism which has ever supported evil upon earth—the attachment of the professional soldier to cruel and obsolete killing machines. I would remind you of the conduct of the Chevalier Bayard, whom his contemporary soldiers described as *sans peur et sans reproche*. To captured knights, and even bowmen, he was the soul of courtesy, but musketeers or other users of gunpowder who fell into his hands were invariably put to death. It is worth remembering that, until the invention of gunpowder, fighting had for many centuries been remarkably safe for everyone who could afford a good suit of armour, while the abominable arquebus and its descendants have saved the remnants of Christendom from the Turks, Mongols, and other paynims who had by Bayard's time successfully overwhelmed one half of its original extent.

I remember an excellent example of Bayardism in the war. A Turkish airman had developed considerable flair for shooting down our observation balloons. A British officer sent up one of these latter with a large cargo of gun-cotton, and blew up the Turk in question. For this deed he was severely reprimanded by the local officer commanding R.A.F. for unsportsmanlike conduct. This gentleman, doubtless, felt little objection to bombing, for example, Turkish transport columns, consisting mainly of noncombatants and animals, incapable of retaliating. (One may remark that between wounds and thirst perhaps 30,000 Turkish transport animals perished during our final victory in Palestine.) But he objected to airmen being killed except by other airmen. I, fighting in the mud beneath them, and exposed to the bombs of both sides (I was severely wounded by one of our own), felt differently. An attempt by the professional soldiers to stereotype the art of war into the channels which correspond to the ideas of 1914 might

CHEMICAL WARFARE

lead to a future rather different from that which I shall venture to predict, a future in which the military organizations of the world were overthrown by the exponents of some other mode of thinking, employing all the resources of science, and fighting "dirty." The opponents of the present world-order may, therefore, welcome Bayardism in their governments.

Meanwhile, the Bayardists have nobbled a curious assortment of allies in their so far successful attempt to prevent the humanization of warfare. First are a number of out-and-out pacifists, who object to all war, and apparently hope to make it more difficult by restricting the means of fighting allowed. Some, of course, genuinely believe that gaseous weapons are more cruel than solid ones. Those who know the facts seem to me to be the victims of loose-thinking. With .them are associated a group of sentimentalists who appear to me definitely to be the Scribes and Pharisees of our age. These people, who are to be found in all political parties and most religious and irreligious sects, are generally willing (after a decent interval) to accept any application of science which appears to them profitable, or any social institution (such as war) which is hallowed by use and wont. They salve their consciences for such behaviour by attacking, in the name of their god or their ideals, every novelty, whether in thought or in action, which presents any loophole. In particular they are distinguished by a ferocious opposition to, and contempt for, any attempt at the solution of human problems by honest and simple intellectual effort. Mustard gas kills one man for every forty it puts out of action; shells kill one for every three; but their god who compromised with high explosives has not yet found time to adapt himself to chemical warfare.

More respectable in every way are the candid reactionaries, like Lord Cecil, who believe in their hearts that in abandoning traditional religion of the medieval type for scientific thought, man has definitely chosen the wrong path, and who fight with their eyes open against its application. These people have a case, and are prepared to argue it. They would honestly desire to give up the gunpowder of Lazare Carnot for

[33]

the sword of Bayard. But one cannot congratulate them on their associates.

And behind these follow like sheep the predestined victims of the next war, the peoples of the civilized nations who will undergo the extremity of suffering rather than think for themselves.

How profound and unreasoning the objection of the military mind to chemical warfare is can best be judged by one simple fact. About three years ago the British regular army gave up the instruction of every soldier in defence against hostile gas. For one thing, speed in adjusting respirators being of more importance than elegance, it did not form the basis of a satisfactory drill, like those curious relics of eighteenth century musketry which still occupy so much of the time of our recruits. But the truth no doubt was that the officers did not like that sort of thing. The chemical and physiological ideas which underlie gas warfare require a certain effort to understand, and they do not arise in the study of a sport, as is the case with those underlying shooting and motor transport. One of the first acts of the late Government was to reinstate some modicum of antigas instruction in the normal training of the Army. But it may be hoped that this pernicious and demoralizing teaching will once more be dropped with the return to power of one of the gentlemen's parties.

Personally, I must confess that I would go very much further than the Government, and seriously consider the provision of gas-masks for the population of London and other large towns, and the instruction of school-children in their use. If this is not done, there is at least the possibility of a disaster of the very first magnitude at an early stage in the next war. It is also one of the very few military measures which could hardly be regarded as provocative by the most ardent of foreign militarists or British pacifists. At the present moment, however, this need does not arise, as the French, who alone could bomb London, have very slight facilities for making mustard gas.

It is interesting to compare the attitude of our militarists to defence against gas with their attitude before the war to a possible German invasion. The fear of the latter, although the naval experts always stated that it was impossible on any serious scale, had been so impressed on the military mind by the propaganda of the National Service League and its like before the war that, from 1914 to 1918 hundreds of thousands of troops were quite unnecessarily kept in England. There is, however, this very fundamental difference between a defence against invasion and a defence against gas. The one would increase the importance of the professional soldier: the other would not. One does not need to be a very profound psychologist to see in this fact one reason why the military authorities dropped anti-gas training, and why I, being a biochemist and therefore a person of the type who would become important if gas war returned, am advocating its extension.

CALLINICUS

As to which of us is justified, I would suggest that it is more likely to-day that poisonous gas will be used against British soldiers or civilians in future wars than it was in 1912 that Britain would be invaded by the Germans.

We have seen that a case can be made out for gas as a weapon on humanitarian grounds, based on the very small proportion of killed to casualties from gas in the war, and especially during its last year. Against this may be urged the probability that future research will produce other gases or smokes which, as weapons, will be as cruel as, or more cruel than, the chlorine and phosgene used in 1915 and 1916. The answer to this is quite simple. First, as regards gases or vapours. Only a limited number of chemical substances are appreciably volatile, and of their vapours only a small proportion are poisonous. Now every chemical substance has a definite molecular weight. Those with a small molecular weight, *i.e.,* whose molecules are relatively light, are on the whole the most volatile, *i.e.,* go most easily into vapour. Now the large majority of the possible volatile chemical substances of small molecular weight, and therefore relatively simple chemical composition, are already known. Mustard gas, for example, was discovered and its properties described in 1886. There are probably substances of high molecular weight whose dense vapours are even more poisonous than mustard gas. But the charcoal of our respirators has the property of adsorbing

[39]

heavy molecules of vapour quite independently of their chemical composition. It is, therefore, somewhat unlikely, though not, of course, impossible, that any very poisonous vapour will ever be found which will go through a mask impermeable to mustard gas or chlorine. It is, to my mind, far more probable that skin irritants may be discovered which are even more unpleasant than mustard gas.

The question of smokes is more serious. It was the hope of the producers of irritant smokes that they would penetrate the gas-masks in sufficient amounts to cause sneezing and force their victims to remove their masks, thus exposing themselves to greater concentrations of smoke and to poisonous vapours liberated along with the smoke. This was the German view when they introduced the "Blue Cross" shell in July, 1917. Fortunately, by that time our defence against gas and smoke was extremely good, and we had foreseen the smoke menace and introduced, between April and June, 1917, a filter which effectively stopped it in the concentrations then met in the field. It is not, however, at all unlikely that concentrations of smoke will be produced in the future which will penetrate our present masks. If our anti-gas measures are sufficiently neglected the consequences may, of course, be very serious.

It would seem likely that the chemical weapons of the future will not be so very unlike those of the past. The main efforts of the soldier who uses them

[41]

will be devoted, first, to blistering his enemy, secondly, to tiring him out by forcing him to wear a respirator continuously, which, of course, enormously hampers him for doing anything else.

In the Great War mustard gas and sensory irritant smokes were not used as the principal weapons of attack or defence, because the smokes would not incapacitate everyone in a given area, though they would make them keep their respirators on. Mustard gas, on the other hand, could make any area absolutely untenable by the defenders, but the vapour persisted for so many days that it could not be occupied by the attackers either. It was mainly used to produce casualties a few days or weeks before an attack on the units which would be defending, and to protect the flank of an offensive against counter-attack. Thus in April, 1918, Armentières, the original Northern limit of the German attack in Flanders, was so heavily shelled with "mustard" that the gutters in the streets were reported to be running with it. The Germans themselves received orders forbidding them to enter its ruins for a fortnight.

Nevertheless, mustard gas is so adequate a weapon that the attempt will almost certainly be made to use it not merely for making ground untenable for both sides, but for gaining it from the enemy. For this purpose the following methods suggest themselves. First, attempts might be made to protect troops completely from the effect of gas on their skins by encasing them

in airtight overalls and gloves. These
were used with a certain amount of
success by machine-gunners in the Great
War, but would hardly be practicable
for attackers, who would, except perhaps in winter, die of heat-stroke if
encased in such apparatus.

Air-tight tanks with adequate arrangements for filtering the incoming
air are probably more hopeful, as
mustard gas will not poison motors as
it does men. (The motors would, of
course, have their own air-supply, as it
would hardly be practicable to filter air
in the quantities needed by them.) To
support the tanks and to tackle specially
protected machine-gunners use will
probably be made of immune infantry.
One attack of gas-poisoning, whether
by the lungs or skin, produces no

immunity to a second attack—in fact, it generally increases the sensitivity of the victim. If a vapour is discovered against which immunity can be conferred, it will be the most effective weapon in history as long as its secret is kept. On the other hand, some people are naturally immune. The American Army authorities made a systematic examination of the susceptibility of large numbers of recruits. They found that there was a very resistant class, comprising 20% of the white men tried, but no less than 80% of the negroes. This is intelligible, as the symptoms of mustard gas, blistering, and sun-burn are very similar, and negroes are pretty well immune to sunburn. It looks therefore as if, after a slight preliminary test, it should be

[45]

possible to obtain coloured troops who would all be resistant to mustard gas blistering in concentrations harmful to most white men. Enough resistant whites are available to officer them.

One sees, then, the possibility of warfare on somewhat the following lines :—

Heavy concentrations of artillery would keep an area say thirty miles in length and ten in depth continuously sprayed with mustard gas. After allowing, say, two days for the development of blisters, the gassing of the positions within two or three miles of the front line is discontinued, but a long-range bombardment, especially of roads, goes on. Suddenly, behind the usual barrage of high explosive shells appears a line of tanks supported by negroes in gas-masks. They meet with but little opposition in the area still reeking of gas, and occupy the hostile lines to a depth of two or three miles. A counter-attack, even if successful, involves concentration in an area under gas-bombardment and enormous casualties from blistering. The only satisfactory counter-attack would be from the air. In this way the side possessing a big superiority of mustard gas should be in a position to advance two or three miles a day.

This kind of tactics was impossible during the Great War for a very simple reason. There was not enough mustard gas. The Germans used a quite surprisingly complicated process for its manufacture. When we decided to follow their example, one of our chemists (a Cambridge man, I am glad to say) hit on a vastly cheaper and speedier method of manufacture. Unfortunately, our first supplies only arrived in the field in September, 1918. There is reason to think that the knowledge that we were at last about to develop gas and smoke warfare on a large scale had a good deal to do with the acceptance by the Germans of the armistice conditions.

The reason why we did not use mustard gas earlier is also simple and rather instructive.

In 1915 a British chemist proposed to a General who was concerned with such questions that the British should use dichlorethyl sulphide. "Does it kill?" asked the General. "No," he was told, "but it will disable enormous

numbers of the enemy temporarily."
"That is no good to us," said the man
of blood; "we want something that
will kill." It is interesting to find how
completely the ideas of this worthy
soldier as to the object of war coincided
with those of the average intelligent
child of five years old. I may remind
you that Clausewitz held the view that
the object of war was to impose one's
will upon the enemy. This idea would,
however, appear to have been too
abstract, too complicated, or too
humanitarian for the British military
mind. At any rate, it had its fill of
killing. It was not, therefore, until the
Germans had demonstrated upon the
persons of some tens of thousands of
British soldiers (we had 14,000 casualties, though with only 400 deaths, dur-

ing the first three weeks of the mustard gas war) that there was something to be said for a weapon that was not primarily designed to kill, that we began to use it.

It seems, then, that mustard gas would enable an army to gain ground with far less killed on either side than the methods used in the late war, and would tend to establish a war of movement leading to a fairly rapid decision, as in the campaigns of the past. It would not much upset the present balance of power, Germany's chemical industry being counterpoised by French negro troops. Indians may be expected to be nearly as immune as negroes.

And clearly, the more war is complicated, the more unimportant become semi-civilized powers, such as Turkey and Russia, even as allies. The Turks were seldom capable of organizing a combined attack by any number greater than a battalion, or a shoot by anything larger than a battery. Yet small groups of them fought very well, and their individual guns made very good shooting. But gas-warfare demands organization, both of attack and defence—attack, because one tries to keep up a certain concentration of vapour over a whole large area rather than to knock out given groups of men; defence, because respirators and discipline in wearing them must be perfect. I need not say that in the Great War our military leaders strongly deprecated the use of gas against the Turks, on the ground, I believe, that the latter were "gentlemen." They showed their gentlemanly character by such acts as the killing of 45% of the prisoners taken at Kut-el-Amara, not to mention some millions of Greeks and Armenians who had the misfortune to be Christians. But they never used gas: so perhaps they may have preserved their quality of gentlemen in the eyes of our Bayardists.

I claim, then, that the use of mustard gas in war on the largest possible scale would render it less expensive of life and property, shorter, and more dependent on brains rather than numbers. We are often told the exact opposite, that it will make it more barbarous and indecisive, and lead to the wiping out of the population of whole cities. Let us consider for a moment this latter allegation. Can aeroplanes do more

[52]

against a hostile town with gas than with high explosive and incendiary bombs? We were threatened with gas bombs during the war, and certain London pharmacists made very large sums by the sale of alleged anti-gas masks. It could be, and was, urged at the time that as the carrying of these curious objects seemed to calm the civilian population in a moment of national emergency, they served a useful purpose. The same argument has been brought forward on behalf of amulets and other pious frauds sold in the name of religion. In the case of the above gas-masks, they inspired such faith (for they had a better finish than the official pattern and looked like one's idea of what a gas-mask ought to be) that some thousands were sent out by fond relatives to soldiers at the front, a number of whom in consequence perished miserably.

Was there anything in the gas-bomb scare? In the first place, many otherwise well-informed people have very erroneous views as to the poisonousness of gases. Gases are dangerous in the laboratory or factory if they kill without giving warning by odour and irritation; but gases of this kind, such as carbon monoxide and hydrogen arsenide, have to be present, in order to kill, in concentrations which cannot practically be produced in the open. The insidiousness of hydrogen arsenide has, however, so alarmed chemists that a tradition persists of a man having been killed by a single bubble of it, while they are so afraid of smelling carbon monoxide that it is generally stated to be inodorous. Besides errors due to this cause, there were errors of arithmetic. In one calculation which was made to show how easily London could be poisoned a decimal point went astray in one place! As the calculation was concerned with volumes of gas, the result came out as 10 metres cubed or 1,000 cubic metres, in place of one. For this reason it appeared that ten aeroplanes could do the damage which would actually have required ten thousand. However, most of the prophets of disaster from gas-bombs made no calculation at all. Let us try to make a rough one. On the nights of March 11th to March 14th, 1918, just before the great offensive of March 21st, the Germans fired 150,000 mustard gas shells into the villages and valleys of the Cambrai salient, an area of about twenty square miles, the same as that of central London. This caused 4,500 casualties, of whom only fifty died (all of them because they took off their respirators too soon). The area was not evacuated. In central London, if the population had had gas-masks, the casualties would have been perhaps ten times greater. But we have to compare this hypothetical air-raid, not with any raid that actually occurred, but with a bombardment of 150,000 high-explosive shells or their equivalent in bombs. This would hardly have left a house in central London untouched, and the dead would have been numbered not in hundreds, but in tens of thousands. Such an attack would have required the visits on repeated nights of something like 1,000 aeroplanes. Such a number is not yet a practical possibility. We are, perhaps, inclined to underestimate the potentialities of town-bombing with high explosive and incendiary bombs. In London, for example, there were never too many big fires started at any given time for the fire-brigades to deal with. An attack by ten or twenty times as many aeroplanes as ever bombed London simultaneously might well ring round a given area fairly completely with wrecked streets or burning houses, in which case most of the buildings and a good proportion of the inhabitants would perish. In one or two air-raids on other towns it seems probable that the Germans were not far from outstripping the capacities of the fire-brigades and producing very large conflagrations.

The reasons why explosives are more likely to be effective than poison on a town are as follows. Houses are far more vulnerable to explosives than earthworks, and do far more damage to their occupants in collapsing, besides being inflammable. And, on the other hand, they contain far more refuges which are nearly gas-proof. A shut room on a first or second floor would be nearly proof against gas released in the neighbourhood if it had not got a lighted fire to drag contaminated air from outside into it. Moreover, civilians could, and would, rapidly evacuate an area which has been heavily soaked with mustard gas, whereas soldiers have to stay on at the risk of their lives.

Gas-bombs would certainly be far less effective than high-explosives on a town whose inhabitants were provided with respirators, probably even if they were unprovided. But, so long as London is undefended in this respect, it constitutes a standing temptation to any power desirous of making this kind of experiment. Judging from experience, there is no doubt that a gas or smoke attack from the air would occasion a first-class panic. The introduction of each new chemical weapon produced great terror, as did even such a militarily unimportant (though cruel) weapon as the *Flammenwerfer* (flame-projector). This was certainly due to ignorance. The French Colonial troops who were caught in the first cloud-gas attack were far more frightened than the Canadians, and appear to have had far more casualties, although they mostly ran away: which the Canadians did not. For the Canadians made some attempts to improvise respirators, and almost any damp fabric will reduce the concentration of chlorine passing through it to half or less. They also breathed less because they did not run. As a matter of fact, a most efficient respirator against chlorine (though whether against mustard gas I do not know) can be made by knocking the bottom off a bottle, filling it with loose earth, placing its neck in the mouth, and breathing through it. Very great alarm was caused by the first mustard gas bombardments in France, as no one

CHEMICAL WARFARE

had ever seen anything resembling the blisters it caused. But very soon familiarity bred contempt, or even liking, for aeroplanes dropped sheaves of pamphlets explaining how any soldier tired of the war could become a casualty without danger either of death or detection by allowing earth contaminated with mustard gas to touch the skin or the clothing. A good many wound-stripes were earned by this simple and up-to-date method, though, as we had the superiority in the air and the German soldiers were both more tired and more confiding than our own, the German casualties from this cause were probably still greater. But let us tell our civilian population before and not after they are attacked with blistering gases that the blisters produced

are considerably less dangerous than
measles. It was predicted during the
war that the survivors of lung-irritant
gases would get consumption, while
those burned by mustard gas would
develop cancer. This has not happened,
but it is the sort of rumour that easily
starts.

For, after all, our greatest weapon in
chemical warfare is not gas, but education, and education of all classes. By
education I mean a process which puts
people in general in touch with the
thought of the abler minds of their own
and past times, whether in literature or
art, in science, mathematics, or music.
An educated man knows enough of
science, for example, to be able to
distinguish a gas from a smoke, or a
Grindell-Matthews from a Marconi,

even if he is not thoroughly versed in the kinetic theory of gases or the laws governing radiation through the ether. Educated men are rather rare. It will be worth while giving some examples of how our uneducated politicians and soldiers failed to adjust themselves to the scientific thought of their contemporaries. In April, 1915, a relatively educated member of the Government got hold of a physiologist, whose name I suppress as he is a modest man. He found a rather curious state of affairs. On the *Emden,* a German cruiser captured in the Indian Ocean, a German sailor had been found in possession of a pad of lint with tapes to tie in front of his mouth. It did not even cover his nose, and, though it might or might not have

been of some value against smoke, it
was of none at all against gas. There
was, however, a very prevalent belief at
that time, and may be still, for all that
I know, that German men of science
were vastly superior to British. It is
perfectly true that there are more of
them, but I think that their average
attainments in the last forty years have
been, if anything, slightly below those
of our own. So hypnotized, however,
were some of the authorities in this
country by this theory that it was being
proposed to issue these articles to our
troops. After pointing out their use-
lessness, the physiologist in question
was rushed over to France in a de-
stroyer, along with a chemist. He
identified the gas used by the Germans
as chlorine. On his return, he got a

cylinder of that gas, let some into an air-tight chamber, and devised a rough respirator which would keep most of it out, trying various possible methods on himself. On his return to the War Office, rather short of breath from the chlorine he had breathed, he found to his horror that the appeal to the women of England for home-made respirators had been issued. Their design was apparently based on the captured German one, which had very probably been made on the *Emden*. As they were quite useless, he secured a promise that they would not be sent out to France. Things were not made easier by the opinion held in high military quarters that, offence being more important than defence, the great thing was to reply to the Germans by gassing them. As, however, this could not be done in less than five months, while respirators could easily be made in a week, it led to delay at a somewhat vital moment. Finally every important decision taken in England had to pass through the hands of Lord Kitchener, who naturally had not time to weigh the arguments at all fully. It is not my intention to attack Lord Kitchener: that the war could be carried on at all under such a system proves that he was a great man. But, if he had managed to delegate some of his powers, he would have proved himself a greater. As the result of all this delay, a great many of the first respirators had to be made in France.

Convalescent soldiers and the nuns in a convent on the Mont des Cats were conscripted to make respirators, which, if inelegant, were fairly efficient. Unfortunately, consignments of "Women of England" and other home-made respirators were continually appearing in France, and every now and then led to a battalion or so being wiped out. I am able to give these details, because at this time I, who before and after was an honest infantry bombing-officer, made my brief incursion into chemical warfare. I arrived at St. Omer from my comfortable trench as being a person accustomed to poisonous gases in civil life. In a large school there, converted into a hospital, there was a small glass-fronted room, like a miniature greenhouse, into which known volumes of chlorine were liberated. We had to compare the effects on ourselves

[67]

of various quantities with and without respirators. It stung the eyes and produced a tendency to gasp and cough when breathed. For this reason trained physiologists had to be employed. An ordinary soldier would probably restrain his tendency to gasp, cough and throw himself about if he were working a machine-gun in a battle, but could not do so in a laboratory experiment vith nothing to take his mind off his own feelings. An experienced physiologist has more self-control. It was also necessary to see if one could run or work hard in the respirators, so we had a wheel of some kind to turn by hand in the gas chamber, not to mention doing fifty-yard sprints in respirators outside. As each of us got sufficiently affected by gas to render his lungs unduly irritable, another would take his place. None of us was much the worse for the gas, or in any real danger, as we knew where to stop, but some had to go to bed for a few days, and I was very short of breath and incapable of running for a month or so. This work, which was mainly done by civilians, was rewarded by the grant of the Military Cross to the brilliant young officer who used to open the door of the motor-car of the medical General who occasionally visited the experiments. The soldiers who took part in them could, however, for some time be distinguished by the peculiar green colour of their brass buttons due to the action of the gas.

Even when arrangements had been made for the manufacture of respira-

tors in England, the supply suddenly
dried up. It was found that the girls
who made them were working as best
they could with raw and bleeding
fingers, and London was being scoured
for rubber gloves. Someone had altered the formula of the mixture in
which the respirators were dipped by
substituting for carbonate of soda caus-
tic soda, which has the property of
dissolving the human skin. His name,
needless to say, does not appear in the
official history.

Such were some of the difficulties
which we incurred in our anti-gas work,
through the ignorance of highly-placed
persons. As, however, our defensive
(though not our offensive) measures
were ultimately better than those of any
other nation, things must have been still

worse elsewhere. The success of our respirators was largely due to one man, Harrison, whose name is insufficiently known to his countrymen. He was an analytical chemist, and author of that admirable and too little read work *Secret Remedies* (published by the British Medical Association). He enlisted as a private, but was a Lieutenant-Colonel when he died of influenza and overwork in 1918. Naturally the ignorance of our private soldiers was of an even more abysmal character. In the early days they often removed the respirators from their faces and tied them around their chests, as it was there that they felt the effects of the gas. Again in 1917 80% of the mustard-gas cases vomited, while this symptom was rare in 1918. Ap-

parently it took five months for the
British Army to realize that gas-poisoning did not necessarily mean poisoning
through the stomach.

If, then, in future wars we are to
avoid gross mismanagement in high
places, and panic and stupidity among
the masses, it is essential that everyone
should learn a little elementary science,
that politicians and soldiers should not
be proud of their ignorance of it, that
ordinary men and women should not
be ashamed or afraid of knowing something of the working of their own
bodies. If we persist in the belief that
we can be saved by patriotism or social
reforms, or by military preparation of
the type which would have sufficed in
former struggles, we shall go down before some nation of more realistic

views. We do not know what type of
scientific knowledge will be needed: we
can be certain that some type will be.
The British are a tired people: they
like to rest "in breathless quiet after all
their ills," and to pin their faith to the
promises of leaders whose eyes are fixed
on the past. It has all happened before.

"Ganz vergessener Völker Müdig-
keiten
Kann ich nicht abthun von meinen
Lidern,
Noch weghalten von der er-
schrockenen Seele
Stummes Niederfallen f e r n e r
Sterne."

("I cannot lift from my eyelids the
weariness of quite forgotten peoples,
nor hold away from my terrified soul
the dumb downfall of far stars.")

[73]

CALLINICUS

The Roman and Spanish Empires appear to have perished largely from intellectual torpor. Are we to go the same way?

We have got to get over our distaste for scientific thought and scientific method. To take an example from the war, the physiologists at the experimental ground at Porton, in Hampshire, had considerable difficulty in working with a good many soldiers because the latter objected so strongly to experiments on animals, and did not conceal their contempt for people who performed them. And yet these soldiers would have had no hesitation in shelling the horses of hostile gun-teams, and the vast majority of them were in the habit of shooting animals for sport. I have never known a physiologist who went in for shooting animals: physiologists know too much of the processes which occur in a wounded beast or bird that creeps away to die. And, though I have seen a good many scientific experiments on animals, I have never seen one which, so far as concerns the pain given, I should object to having performed on myself. That this attitude is not unusual would appear from the following experiment described by the director of the Porton experimental ground, in which he wished to compare the effects of hydrocyanic (or prussic) acid gas on himself and a dog. They both entered a chamber containing 1 part in 2,000 of the gas.

"In order (he writes) that the experiment might be as fair as possible and that my respiration should be relatively as active as that of the dog, I remained standing, and took a few steps from time to time while I was in the chamber. In about thirty seconds the dog began to get unsteady, and in fifty-five seconds it dropped on the floor and commenced the characteristic distressing respiration which heralds death from cyanide poisoning. One minute thirty-five seconds after the commencement the animal's body was carried out, respiration having ceased and the dog being apparently dead. I then left the chamber. As regards the result upon myself, the only real effect was a momentary giddiness when I turned my head quickly. This lasted about a year, and then vanished. For some time it was difficult to concentrate on anything for any length of time. It is hard to say to what extent this was due to the experiment."

As the result of this work, hydrocyanic acid was given up for use in the field, as phosgene is effective at fifty times this dilution, and mustard gas at one thousand times.

One of the grounds given for objection to science is that science is responsible for such horrors as those of the late war. "You scientific men (we are told) never think of the possible application of your discoveries. You do not mind whether they are used to kill or to cure. Your method of thinking, doubtless satisfactory when dealing with molecules and atoms, renders you insensible to the difference between right and wrong. And so you devise the means of universal destruction, and

[77]

sell them into the hands of unrighteous and bloody-minded men."

I note that the people who make these remarks do not refuse to travel by railway or motor-car, to use electric light, or to read mechanically printed newspapers. Nor do they install a well in their back-gardens to enjoy drinking the richer water of a pre-scientific age, with its interesting and variegated fauna. But it is quite easy to show that the destructive and horrible nature of modern warfare is due, not to the weapons used, but largely to the other applications of science which constitute the material basis of our civilization. Let us imagine the Great War fought with all our means of transport and preventive medicine, but no weapons more complicated than swords, spears, and possibly a few bows. With fewer munitions the armies could have been mobilized even more rapidly, and more men put in the fighting line. The Germans would probably have tried, as they tried in 1914, to bring about a "Schlacht ohne Morgen," a battle on reversed fronts modelled on Cannae. The fighting would probably have been about as severe as at Cannae, and men would have been fighting in close order, ten or twenty deep, along a hundred-mile front. No doubt it would have been over sooner, but the losses would probably have been just as great. The French and Germans would doubtless both have gone on fighting until at least half their armies had become casualties, and, with four years' fighting compressed into as many weeks, it would have been impossible to tend more than a fraction of the wounded. The chief difference might have been that the Russians would have been victorious by mere weight of numbers, and the French defeated. In former wars slaughter was limited by the fact that large armies could not be fed, and developed epidemic diseases. They also moved very slowly. So it took twenty-three years (from 1792 to 1815) to wear down the resistance of the French nation. Moreover, the Great War was the first since the Second Punic War of the 3rd century B. C. between two great civilized nations, each fighting with all its might. This fact accounts for its ferocity. Modern transport and hygiene made its scale possible; the weapons used merely served to prolong it.

CHEMICAL WARFARE

The objection to scientific weapons such as the gases of the late war, and such new devices as may be employed in the next, is essentially an objection to the unknown. Fighting with lances or guns, one can calculate, or thinks one can calculate, one's chances. But with gas or rays or microbes one has an altogether different state of affairs. Poisonous gas had a great moral effect, just because it was new, and incomprehensible. As long as we permit ourselves to be afraid of the novel and unknown, there will be a very great temptation to use novel and unknown weapons against us. Now, terror of the unknown is thoroughly right and rational so long as we believe that the prince of this world is a malignant being. But it is not justifiable if we believe that the world is the expression of a power friendly to our aspirations, or if we are atheists and hold that it is neutral and indifferent to human ideals.

It will by now have become clear to you that I am writing somewhat parabolically. What I have said about mustard gas might be applied, *mutatis mutandis,* to most other applications of science to human life. They can all, I think, be abused, but none perhaps is always evil; and many, like mustard gas, when we have got over our first not very rational objection to them, turn out to be, on the whole, good. If it is right for me to fight my enemy with a sword, it is right for me to fight him with mustard gas: if the one is wrong, so is the other. But I have no sympathy whatever for Mr. Facing-both-ways when he says that, though he is prepared on occasion to fight, he will not use these nasty new-fangled weapons. Of course I am not suggesting that we should violate or prepare to violate the Washington Agreement on this subject. I do, however, believe that we ought to denounce it at the earliest possible opportunity.

Such are the facts about chemical warfare. They will not be believed because a belief in them would do violence to the sentiments of most people. They will not be promulgated, as there is no money to be made out of them. (Chemical manufacturers make both high explosive and mustard gas, and the former more easily.) The views which I have expressed do not coexist in the mind of any party leader

[83]

or newspaper proprietor, and must
therefore be those of a crank. But
until some stronger argument can be
waged against them than that they are
unusual and unpleasant, there remains
the possibility that they are true.

DATE DUE

DEC 10			
OC1 3			
NO 29 '99			

DEMCO 38-297